# 50 Premium Seafood Recipes

By: Kelly Johnson

# Table of Contents

- Lobster Thermidor
- Seared Scallops with Lemon Butter
- Crab Cakes with Aioli
- Grilled Swordfish Steaks
- Shrimp Scampi
- Baked Chilean Sea Bass
- Oysters Rockefeller
- Seafood Paella
- Tuna Tartare
- Blackened Redfish
- Bouillabaisse
- Miso-Glazed Black Cod
- Clam Chowder
- Grilled Octopus
- Lobster Bisque
- Crab-Stuffed Mushrooms
- Sautéed Jumbo Shrimp

- Pan-Seared Halibut
- Salmon en Papillote
- Fried Soft-Shell Crab
- Ceviche
- Lobster Mac and Cheese
- Scallop Risotto
- Mussels in White Wine Sauce
- Tuna Niçoise Salad
- Grilled Prawns with Garlic
- Seafood Linguine
- Smoked Salmon Canapés
- Crab Rangoon
- Pan-Roasted Sea Bass
- Seafood Stir-Fry
- Lobster Rolls
- Crab and Avocado Salad
- Grilled Mahi Mahi
- Tuna Steak with Sesame Crust
- Clams Casino

- Lobster and Corn Chowder
- Shrimp and Grits
- Fried Calamari
- Salmon Tartare
- Blackened Catfish
- Seafood Gumbo
- Lobster Salad with Citrus Vinaigrette
- Crab Pasta with Garlic and Herbs
- Baked Oysters with Parmesan
- Grilled Shrimp Skewers
- Lobster Ravioli
- Pan-Seared Trout
- Seafood Casserole
- Smoked Trout Dip

## Lobster Thermidor

**Ingredients:**

- 2 cooked lobster tails, meat removed
- 2 tbsp butter
- 1 shallot, minced
- 1 garlic clove, minced
- 1/2 cup mushrooms, chopped
- 1/2 cup heavy cream
- 1 tbsp Dijon mustard
- 1/4 cup Parmesan cheese, grated
- Fresh tarragon, chopped
- Salt and pepper
- Paprika for garnish

**Instructions:**

1. Preheat oven to 375°F (190°C).
2. Sauté shallots, garlic, and mushrooms in butter until soft.
3. Stir in cream, mustard, tarragon; cook until slightly thickened.
4. Chop lobster meat, add to sauce, season with salt and pepper.
5. Spoon mixture into lobster shells, top with Parmesan and paprika.

6. Bake 10-12 minutes until golden and bubbly.

## Seared Scallops with Lemon Butter

### Ingredients:

- 12 large sea scallops
- Salt and pepper
- 2 tbsp olive oil
- 3 tbsp butter
- Juice of 1 lemon
- Fresh parsley, chopped

### Instructions:

1. Pat scallops dry, season with salt and pepper.
2. Heat olive oil in skillet over high heat.
3. Sear scallops 2-3 min per side until golden crust forms.
4. Remove scallops, reduce heat, add butter and lemon juice.
5. Pour lemon butter over scallops, garnish with parsley.

## Crab Cakes with Aioli

### Ingredients:

- 1 lb crab meat
- 1/2 cup breadcrumbs
- 1 egg, beaten
- 2 tbsp mayonnaise
- 1 tbsp Dijon mustard
- 1 tbsp fresh parsley, chopped
- Salt and pepper
- Oil for frying

### Aioli:

- 1/2 cup mayonnaise
- 1 garlic clove, minced
- 1 tbsp lemon juice
- Salt to taste

### Instructions:

1. Mix crab, breadcrumbs, egg, mayo, mustard, parsley, salt, and pepper.
2. Form into patties, chill 30 min.
3. Fry in hot oil 3-4 min per side until golden.

4. Mix aioli ingredients, serve alongside crab cakes.

**Grilled Swordfish Steaks**

**Ingredients:**

- 4 swordfish steaks
- Olive oil
- Salt and pepper
- Lemon wedges
- Fresh herbs (thyme or rosemary)

**Instructions:**

1. Brush swordfish with olive oil, season.
2. Grill on medium-high 4-5 min per side until opaque.
3. Serve with lemon wedges and herbs.

## Shrimp Scampi

**Ingredients:**

- 1 lb large shrimp, peeled and deveined
- 4 tbsp butter
- 3 cloves garlic, minced
- 1/4 cup white wine or chicken broth
- Juice of 1 lemon
- Red pepper flakes (optional)
- Parsley, chopped
- Salt and pepper

**Instructions:**

1. Melt butter, sauté garlic until fragrant.
2. Add shrimp, cook until pink.
3. Pour in wine, lemon juice, and red pepper flakes; simmer 2 min.
4. Season, garnish with parsley.

**Baked Chilean Sea Bass**

**Ingredients:**

- 4 sea bass fillets
- Olive oil
- Salt and pepper
- Lemon slices
- Fresh dill or parsley

**Instructions:**

1. Preheat oven to 400°F (200°C).
2. Brush fillets with olive oil, season.
3. Place lemon slices on top, bake 12-15 min until flaky.
4. Garnish with herbs.

## Oysters Rockefeller

**Ingredients:**

- 12 fresh oysters, shucked
- 2 cups spinach, chopped
- 1/4 cup parsley, chopped
- 2 green onions, chopped
- 1/2 cup breadcrumbs
- 1/4 cup Parmesan cheese
- 3 tbsp butter
- 1 garlic clove, minced
- Salt and pepper

**Instructions:**

1. Preheat broiler.
2. Sauté spinach, parsley, green onions, and garlic in butter until wilted.
3. Mix in breadcrumbs and Parmesan.
4. Spoon mixture onto oysters, place on baking sheet.
5. Broil 3-5 min until topping is golden.

**Seafood Paella**

**Ingredients:**

- 1 1/2 cups Arborio or paella rice
- 4 cups seafood stock
- 1/2 lb shrimp
- 1/2 lb mussels or clams
- 1/2 lb squid rings
- 1 onion, chopped
- 1 bell pepper, chopped
- 2 garlic cloves, minced
- 1 tsp smoked paprika
- Saffron threads (optional)
- Olive oil
- Salt and pepper
- Fresh parsley and lemon wedges

**Instructions:**

1. Heat olive oil, sauté onion, bell pepper, and garlic.
2. Add rice, stir to coat.
3. Pour in stock with saffron, paprika; simmer uncovered.

4. When rice is halfway cooked, add seafood.

5. Cook until seafood is done and liquid absorbed.

6. Season, garnish with parsley and lemon.

## Tuna Tartare

### Ingredients:

- 8 oz fresh sushi-grade tuna, finely diced
- 1 tbsp soy sauce
- 1 tsp sesame oil
- 1 tsp fresh lime juice
- 1 tsp grated fresh ginger
- 1 green onion, finely chopped
- 1 tbsp fresh cilantro, chopped
- Salt and black pepper, to taste
- Optional: 1/4 cup diced avocado or cucumber

### Instructions:

1. In a mixing bowl, combine the diced tuna, soy sauce, sesame oil, lime juice, and grated ginger.
2. Add the chopped green onion and cilantro.
3. Gently fold in diced avocado or cucumber if using.
4. Season with salt and pepper to taste.
5. Chill for at least 15 minutes before serving.
6. Serve with crackers, crostini, or as is.

## Blackened Redfish

### Ingredients:

- 4 redfish fillets (about 6 oz each)
- 2 tbsp blackened seasoning (mix paprika, cayenne pepper, garlic powder, onion powder, dried thyme, dried oregano, salt, and pepper)
- 2 tbsp olive oil
- Lemon wedges for serving

### Instructions:

1. Pat the redfish fillets dry with paper towels.
2. Evenly coat each fillet with blackened seasoning on both sides.
3. Heat olive oil in a heavy skillet over medium-high heat until hot but not smoking.
4. Add the fillets and cook 3-4 minutes per side until blackened and cooked through.
5. Serve immediately with lemon wedges.

**Bouillabaisse**

**Ingredients:**

- 1 lb mixed fish fillets (such as cod, snapper)
- 1 lb shellfish (mussels, clams, shrimp)
- 2 tbsp olive oil
- 1 large onion, chopped
- 2 garlic cloves, minced
- 1 fennel bulb, sliced thin
- 2 large ripe tomatoes, diced
- 4 cups fish stock or seafood broth
- 1/2 cup dry white wine
- A pinch of saffron threads
- 1 bay leaf
- 1 tsp fresh thyme or 1/2 tsp dried
- Salt and pepper to taste
- Fresh parsley, chopped for garnish

**Instructions:**

1. Heat olive oil in a large pot over medium heat. Sauté the onion, garlic, and fennel until softened, about 5 minutes.

2. Add diced tomatoes and cook for 5 more minutes until they break down.

3. Pour in fish stock and white wine, then add saffron, bay leaf, and thyme. Bring to a simmer.

4. Simmer the broth for 20 minutes to develop flavors.

5. Add fish and shellfish. Cover and cook until shellfish open and fish is opaque, about 5-7 minutes. Discard any unopened shellfish.

6. Season with salt and pepper. Remove bay leaf.

7. Serve hot, garnished with parsley.

## Miso-Glazed Black Cod

**Ingredients:**

- 4 black cod fillets (about 6 oz each)
- 1/4 cup white miso paste
- 2 tbsp mirin
- 2 tbsp sake
- 1 tbsp granulated sugar

**Instructions:**

1. In a bowl, whisk together the miso paste, mirin, sake, and sugar until smooth.
2. Place the cod fillets in a shallow dish and coat them evenly with the marinade. Cover and refrigerate for at least 2 hours, preferably overnight.
3. Preheat the broiler to high.
4. Remove excess marinade from the fillets and place them skin-side down on a foil-lined baking sheet.
5. Broil for 8-10 minutes or until the fish is caramelized on top and flakes easily with a fork.
6. Serve immediately.

**Clam Chowder**

**Ingredients:**

- 2 cups chopped clams with juice reserved
- 4 slices bacon, chopped
- 1 large onion, diced
- 2 celery stalks, diced
- 2 medium potatoes, peeled and diced
- 2 cups clam juice and seafood broth (or substitute all broth)
- 1 cup heavy cream
- 2 tbsp unsalted butter
- Salt and pepper to taste
- Fresh thyme or parsley for garnish

**Instructions:**

1. In a large pot, cook bacon over medium heat until crisp. Remove bacon pieces and set aside, leaving fat in the pot.

2. Add onion and celery to the pot and sauté in bacon fat until soft, about 5 minutes.

3. Add diced potatoes, clam juice, and seafood broth. Bring to a simmer and cook until potatoes are tender, about 15 minutes.

4. Stir in clams, heavy cream, butter, and cooked bacon. Heat gently until warmed through but do not boil.

5. Season with salt and pepper to taste.

6. Garnish with fresh thyme or parsley before serving.

## Grilled Octopus

### Ingredients:

- 2 lbs octopus, cleaned
- Juice of 1 lemon
- 4 cloves garlic, minced
- 1/4 cup olive oil
- Salt and freshly ground black pepper
- Fresh parsley, chopped for garnish

### Instructions:

1. Bring a large pot of salted water to a boil. Add the octopus and simmer gently until tender when pierced with a fork, about 45-60 minutes. Drain and let cool.
2. Cut the octopus into serving-sized pieces.
3. In a bowl, whisk together lemon juice, garlic, olive oil, salt, and pepper. Toss the octopus pieces in the marinade and let sit for 30 minutes.
4. Preheat a grill or grill pan over medium-high heat.
5. Grill octopus pieces for 3-4 minutes per side until charred and heated through.
6. Garnish with fresh parsley and serve.

## Lobster Bisque

**Ingredients:**

- 2 lobster tails
- 4 tbsp unsalted butter
- 1 onion, chopped
- 2 carrots, diced
- 2 celery stalks, diced
- 2 cloves garlic, minced
- 1/4 cup brandy or dry sherry
- 4 cups seafood stock
- 1 cup heavy cream
- Salt and freshly ground black pepper
- Paprika and chopped chives for garnish

**Instructions:**

1. Remove lobster meat from tails and chop into bite-sized pieces. Reserve shells.
2. In a large pot, melt butter over medium heat. Add onion, carrots, celery, and garlic; cook until softened, about 8 minutes.
3. Add lobster shells and cook for 5 minutes to release flavor.
4. Carefully add brandy and cook until mostly evaporated.
5. Add seafood stock, bring to a boil, then reduce heat and simmer for 30 minutes.

6. Strain broth through a fine sieve, discard solids. Return broth to pot.

7. Stir in heavy cream and lobster meat. Heat gently until lobster is cooked through, about 5 minutes.

8. Season with salt and pepper.

9. Serve hot, garnished with paprika and chives.

## Crab-Stuffed Mushrooms

### Ingredients:

- 16 large mushroom caps, stems removed
- 1 cup fresh crab meat
- 1/4 cup breadcrumbs
- 2 tbsp mayonnaise
- 1 tbsp Dijon mustard
- 1 green onion, finely chopped
- 1/4 cup grated Parmesan cheese
- Salt and freshly ground black pepper
- Olive oil for drizzling

### Instructions:

1. Preheat oven to 375°F (190°C).
2. In a bowl, combine crab meat, breadcrumbs, mayonnaise, Dijon mustard, green onion, salt, and pepper. Mix gently.
3. Stuff each mushroom cap with the crab mixture.
4. Place stuffed mushrooms on a baking sheet and sprinkle Parmesan cheese over the tops.
5. Drizzle lightly with olive oil.
6. Bake for 15-20 minutes, until the mushrooms are tender and the topping is golden brown.

7. Serve warm.

**Sautéed Jumbo Shrimp**

**Ingredients:**

- 1 lb jumbo shrimp, peeled and deveined
- 3 tbsp olive oil
- 4 cloves garlic, minced
- 1/4 tsp red pepper flakes (optional)
- Juice of 1 lemon
- Salt and pepper, to taste
- Fresh parsley, chopped for garnish

**Instructions:**

1. Heat olive oil in a large skillet over medium-high heat.
2. Add garlic and red pepper flakes; sauté until fragrant, about 30 seconds.
3. Add shrimp in a single layer, season with salt and pepper.
4. Cook shrimp 2-3 minutes per side until pink and opaque.
5. Remove from heat and squeeze lemon juice over shrimp.
6. Garnish with parsley and serve immediately.

**Pan-Seared Halibut**

**Ingredients:**

- 4 halibut fillets (6 oz each)
- Salt and freshly ground black pepper
- 2 tbsp olive oil
- 2 tbsp unsalted butter
- 2 cloves garlic, smashed
- 1 sprig fresh thyme or rosemary
- Lemon wedges for serving

**Instructions:**

1. Pat halibut dry and season both sides with salt and pepper.
2. Heat olive oil in a skillet over medium-high heat.
3. Add halibut fillets skin-side down and cook for 4-5 minutes without moving.
4. Flip fillets and add butter, garlic, and herbs to the pan.
5. Spoon the melted butter over the fish while cooking for another 3-4 minutes until cooked through.
6. Serve with lemon wedges.

**Salmon en Papillote**

**Ingredients:**

- 4 salmon fillets
- 1 lemon, thinly sliced
- 1 zucchini, thinly sliced
- 1 carrot, thinly sliced
- 1/2 cup cherry tomatoes, halved
- 2 tbsp olive oil
- Salt and pepper, to taste
- Fresh dill or parsley for garnish
- Parchment paper or foil

**Instructions:**

1. Preheat oven to 400°F (200°C).
2. Cut 4 large sheets of parchment paper or foil.
3. Place salmon fillet in the center of each sheet.
4. Top with lemon slices, zucchini, carrot, and cherry tomatoes.
5. Drizzle with olive oil and season with salt and pepper.
6. Fold the parchment paper over the salmon and vegetables to create a sealed packet.

7. Place packets on a baking sheet and bake for 12-15 minutes, until salmon is cooked through.

8. Carefully open packets, garnish with fresh dill or parsley, and serve.

## Fried Soft-Shell Crab

**Ingredients:**

- 4 soft-shell crabs, cleaned
- 1 cup all-purpose flour
- 1/2 cup cornmeal
- 1 tsp Old Bay seasoning
- Salt and pepper, to taste
- 2 eggs, beaten
- Vegetable oil, for frying
- Lemon wedges for serving

**Instructions:**

1. Mix flour, cornmeal, Old Bay seasoning, salt, and pepper in a shallow dish.
2. Dip each crab into beaten eggs, then dredge in flour mixture.
3. Heat about 2 inches of vegetable oil in a deep skillet to 350°F (175°C).
4. Fry crabs for 3-4 minutes per side until golden brown and crispy.
5. Drain on paper towels and serve with lemon wedges.

## Ceviche

**Ingredients:**

- 1 lb fresh firm white fish (like snapper or sea bass), diced
- Juice of 5 limes
- 1/2 red onion, thinly sliced
- 1 jalapeño, seeded and minced
- 1 cup diced tomatoes
- 1/4 cup chopped fresh cilantro
- Salt and pepper, to taste
- Tortilla chips or tostadas for serving

**Instructions:**

1. Place diced fish in a glass or ceramic bowl.
2. Pour lime juice over fish to cover completely. Cover and refrigerate for 2-3 hours, until fish is opaque.
3. Drain most of the lime juice, leaving a little for flavor.
4. Stir in red onion, jalapeño, tomatoes, and cilantro.
5. Season with salt and pepper.
6. Serve chilled with tortilla chips or tostadas.

**Lobster Mac and Cheese**

**Ingredients:**

- 8 oz elbow macaroni
- 2 cups cooked lobster meat, chopped
- 3 tbsp unsalted butter
- 3 tbsp all-purpose flour
- 2 cups milk
- 1 cup shredded sharp cheddar cheese
- 1 cup shredded Gruyère cheese
- 1/2 cup grated Parmesan cheese
- Salt and pepper, to taste
- 1/2 cup breadcrumbs (optional)

**Instructions:**

1. Cook macaroni according to package instructions; drain and set aside.
2. In a saucepan, melt butter over medium heat. Whisk in flour and cook for 1-2 minutes.
3. Slowly whisk in milk and cook until thickened, about 5 minutes.
4. Remove from heat and stir in cheddar, Gruyère, and Parmesan until melted. Season with salt and pepper.
5. Add cooked macaroni and lobster meat, mix well.

6. Pour into a baking dish, top with breadcrumbs if using.

7. Broil for 3-5 minutes until golden and bubbly.

8. Serve hot.

## Scallop Risotto

### Ingredients:

- 1 lb sea scallops
- 1 cup Arborio rice
- 4 cups chicken or vegetable broth, kept warm
- 1 small onion, finely chopped
- 2 cloves garlic, minced
- 1/2 cup dry white wine
- 3 tbsp unsalted butter
- 1/2 cup grated Parmesan cheese
- Olive oil
- Salt and pepper, to taste
- Fresh parsley for garnish

### Instructions:

1. Heat olive oil in a skillet over medium-high heat. Season scallops with salt and pepper and sear for 2-3 minutes per side until golden. Remove and set aside.

2. In a large saucepan, melt 1 tbsp butter and sauté onion and garlic until translucent.

3. Add Arborio rice and toast for 1-2 minutes.

4. Pour in white wine and stir until absorbed.

5. Gradually add warm broth, one ladle at a time, stirring constantly, waiting until each ladle is absorbed before adding the next. Continue until rice is creamy and al dente, about 18-20 minutes.

6. Stir in remaining butter and Parmesan cheese. Adjust salt and pepper.

7. Plate risotto and top with seared scallops. Garnish with parsley.

**Mussels in White Wine Sauce**

**Ingredients:**

- 2 lbs fresh mussels, cleaned and debearded
- 2 tbsp olive oil
- 4 cloves garlic, minced
- 1 shallot, minced
- 1 cup dry white wine
- 1/2 cup chopped fresh parsley
- 2 tbsp unsalted butter
- Salt and pepper, to taste
- Lemon wedges for serving

**Instructions:**

1. Heat olive oil in a large pot over medium heat. Sauté garlic and shallot until fragrant and translucent.
2. Add mussels and pour in white wine. Cover pot and steam for 5-7 minutes, shaking the pot occasionally, until mussels open.
3. Discard any unopened mussels.
4. Stir in butter and parsley. Season with salt and pepper.
5. Serve immediately with lemon wedges and crusty bread to soak up the sauce.

**Tuna Niçoise Salad**

**Ingredients:**

- 2 tuna steaks (6 oz each)
- 4 cups mixed salad greens
- 1 cup green beans, blanched
- 1 cup cherry tomatoes, halved
- 1/2 cup black olives
- 4 hard-boiled eggs, halved
- 1/2 cup small boiled potatoes, halved
- 1/4 cup red onion, thinly sliced
- Olive oil, for grilling and dressing
- 1 tbsp Dijon mustard
- 1 tbsp red wine vinegar
- Salt and pepper, to taste

**Instructions:**

1. Season tuna steaks with salt and pepper. Heat olive oil in a grill pan and sear tuna 2-3 minutes per side for medium-rare. Let rest, then slice.
2. In a bowl, whisk Dijon mustard, red wine vinegar, 3 tbsp olive oil, salt, and pepper to make the dressing.
3. Arrange greens on a platter; top with green beans, tomatoes, olives, potatoes, onion, and eggs.

4. Place tuna slices on top and drizzle with dressing. Serve immediately.

**Grilled Prawns with Garlic**

**Ingredients:**

- 1 lb large prawns, peeled and deveined
- 4 cloves garlic, minced
- 3 tbsp olive oil
- Juice of 1 lemon
- 1 tsp smoked paprika
- Salt and pepper, to taste
- Fresh parsley, chopped for garnish

**Instructions:**

1. In a bowl, combine garlic, olive oil, lemon juice, smoked paprika, salt, and pepper. Add prawns and marinate for 20 minutes.
2. Preheat grill or grill pan to medium-high heat.
3. Thread prawns onto skewers and grill 2-3 minutes per side until opaque.
4. Garnish with parsley and serve hot.

**Seafood Linguine**

**Ingredients:**

- 8 oz linguine pasta
- 2 tbsp olive oil
- 2 cloves garlic, minced
- 1/2 tsp red pepper flakes
- 1/2 lb shrimp, peeled and deveined
- 1/2 lb mussels, cleaned
- 1/2 lb scallops
- 1 cup cherry tomatoes, halved
- 1/2 cup white wine
- 1/4 cup chopped fresh parsley
- Salt and pepper, to taste

**Instructions:**

1. Cook linguine according to package instructions; drain and set aside.
2. Heat olive oil in a large skillet, sauté garlic and red pepper flakes until fragrant.
3. Add shrimp and scallops, cook 2-3 minutes until just opaque. Remove and set aside.
4. Add mussels and white wine, cover and cook 3-4 minutes until mussels open. Discard any unopened.

5. Return shrimp and scallops to pan; add cherry tomatoes and parsley. Toss with linguine, season with salt and pepper. Serve immediately.

## Smoked Salmon Canapés

### Ingredients:

- 8 oz smoked salmon, sliced
- 1 baguette, sliced into rounds and toasted
- 4 oz cream cheese, softened
- 1 tbsp fresh dill, chopped
- 1 tbsp lemon juice
- Capers for garnish
- Fresh dill sprigs for garnish

### Instructions:

1. Mix cream cheese, lemon juice, and chopped dill until smooth.
2. Spread cream cheese mixture on toasted baguette slices.
3. Top each with a slice of smoked salmon.
4. Garnish with capers and dill sprigs. Serve chilled.

**Crab Rangoon**

**Ingredients:**

- 8 oz cream cheese, softened
- 1 cup cooked crab meat, finely chopped
- 2 green onions, finely chopped
- 1 tsp soy sauce
- 1/2 tsp garlic powder
- Wonton wrappers
- Vegetable oil for frying

**Instructions:**

1. In a bowl, combine cream cheese, crab meat, green onions, soy sauce, and garlic powder.
2. Place a teaspoon of filling in the center of each wonton wrapper.
3. Moisten edges with water, fold to seal into triangles or purses.
4. Heat oil in a deep skillet to 350°F (175°C). Fry crab rangoons in batches until golden, about 2-3 minutes.
5. Drain on paper towels and serve with sweet chili sauce.

**Pan-Roasted Sea Bass**

**Ingredients:**

- 4 sea bass fillets
- Salt and pepper, to taste
- 2 tbsp olive oil
- 2 tbsp unsalted butter
- 2 cloves garlic, smashed
- 1 sprig rosemary or thyme
- Lemon wedges for serving

**Instructions:**

1. Season sea bass with salt and pepper.
2. Heat olive oil in an oven-safe skillet over medium-high heat.
3. Place sea bass skin-side down and cook 4-5 minutes until crispy.
4. Flip fish, add butter, garlic, and herbs to pan. Spoon butter over fish while cooking for 3-4 minutes.
5. Transfer skillet to a preheated 400°F oven for 3-5 minutes to finish cooking.
6. Serve with lemon wedges.

## Seafood Stir-Fry

### Ingredients:

- 1/2 lb shrimp, peeled and deveined
- 1/2 lb scallops
- 1/2 lb squid rings
- 2 tbsp vegetable oil
- 3 cloves garlic, minced
- 1 bell pepper, sliced
- 1 cup snap peas
- 2 tbsp soy sauce
- 1 tbsp oyster sauce
- 1 tsp grated fresh ginger
- Cooked jasmine rice, for serving

### Instructions:

1. Heat oil in a wok or large skillet over high heat.
2. Add garlic and ginger, stir-fry until fragrant.
3. Add shrimp, scallops, and squid; stir-fry until just cooked, about 3-4 minutes. Remove and set aside.
4. Add bell pepper and snap peas, stir-fry 2 minutes.

5. Return seafood to pan, add soy sauce and oyster sauce, toss to coat and heat through.

6. Serve over jasmine rice.

## Lobster Rolls

### Ingredients:

- 1 lb cooked lobster meat, chopped
- 1/4 cup mayonnaise
- 1 tbsp lemon juice
- 1 tbsp finely chopped celery
- 1 tbsp finely chopped chives
- Salt and pepper, to taste
- 4 split-top hot dog buns
- 2 tbsp butter, for toasting buns
- Lettuce leaves (optional)

### Instructions:

1. In a bowl, mix lobster meat, mayonnaise, lemon juice, celery, chives, salt, and pepper.
2. Butter the outside of buns and toast in a skillet until golden brown.
3. Line buns with lettuce leaves if desired.
4. Fill buns with lobster mixture and serve immediately.

**Crab and Avocado Salad**

**Ingredients:**

- 1 cup lump crab meat
- 1 large avocado, diced
- 1 cup cherry tomatoes, halved
- 1/4 cup red onion, finely chopped
- 1 tbsp fresh cilantro, chopped
- Juice of 1 lime
- 2 tbsp olive oil
- Salt and pepper, to taste

**Instructions:**

1. In a large bowl, gently toss crab meat, avocado, tomatoes, red onion, and cilantro.
2. In a small bowl, whisk lime juice, olive oil, salt, and pepper.
3. Drizzle dressing over salad and toss gently to combine. Serve chilled.

**Grilled Mahi Mahi**

**Ingredients:**

- 4 mahi mahi fillets (6 oz each)
- 3 tbsp olive oil
- 2 cloves garlic, minced
- Juice of 1 lemon
- 1 tsp smoked paprika
- Salt and pepper, to taste
- Fresh parsley, chopped for garnish

**Instructions:**

1. In a bowl, combine olive oil, garlic, lemon juice, paprika, salt, and pepper.
2. Marinate mahi mahi fillets in the mixture for 15-20 minutes.
3. Preheat grill to medium-high heat.
4. Grill fish 4-5 minutes per side until cooked through and flaky.
5. Garnish with parsley and serve with lemon wedges.

**Tuna Steak with Sesame Crust**

**Ingredients:**

- 2 tuna steaks (6 oz each)
- 1/4 cup sesame seeds (black, white, or mixed)
- 2 tbsp soy sauce
- 1 tbsp sesame oil
- 1 tbsp olive oil
- Salt and pepper, to taste

**Instructions:**

1. Brush tuna steaks with soy sauce and sesame oil.
2. Press sesame seeds evenly onto both sides of the steaks.
3. Heat olive oil in a skillet over medium-high heat.
4. Sear tuna steaks 1-2 minutes per side for rare, or longer to desired doneness.
5. Slice and serve immediately.

## Clams Casino

**Ingredients:**

- 12 fresh clams, scrubbed
- 4 slices bacon, cooked and crumbled
- 1/4 cup red bell pepper, finely diced
- 2 cloves garlic, minced
- 2 tbsp butter
- 1/4 cup breadcrumbs
- 2 tbsp parsley, chopped
- Lemon wedges, for serving

**Instructions:**

1. Preheat broiler.
2. Steam clams until they just open, remove top shells and set clams aside.
3. In a skillet, melt butter and sauté garlic and bell pepper until softened.
4. Mix breadcrumbs, bacon, parsley, and sautéed vegetables.
5. Spoon mixture on top of each clam, place on baking sheet.
6. Broil 2-3 minutes until topping is golden and crisp. Serve with lemon wedges.

**Lobster and Corn Chowder**

**Ingredients:**

- 1 lb cooked lobster meat, chopped
- 4 slices bacon, diced
- 1 onion, diced
- 2 cloves garlic, minced
- 3 cups corn kernels (fresh or frozen)
- 3 cups potatoes, peeled and diced
- 4 cups chicken or seafood stock
- 1 cup heavy cream
- Salt and pepper, to taste
- Fresh chives, chopped for garnish

**Instructions:**

1. In a large pot, cook bacon until crisp. Remove and set aside.
2. In bacon fat, sauté onion and garlic until translucent.
3. Add potatoes, corn, and stock; bring to a boil, then simmer until potatoes are tender (about 15 minutes).
4. Stir in cream and lobster meat; heat through gently.
5. Season with salt and pepper, garnish with bacon and chives. Serve hot.

## Shrimp and Grits

### Ingredients:

- 1 cup stone-ground grits
- 4 cups water
- 1 cup shredded sharp cheddar cheese
- 2 tbsp butter
- 1 lb shrimp, peeled and deveined
- 4 slices bacon, diced
- 1 clove garlic, minced
- 1/2 cup green onions, sliced
- 1 tbsp lemon juice
- Salt and pepper, to taste

### Instructions:

1. Bring water to a boil; slowly whisk in grits. Reduce heat and cook until thickened, about 25-30 minutes. Stir often.
2. Stir in butter and cheese; season with salt and pepper. Keep warm.
3. In a skillet, cook bacon until crisp; remove and set aside.
4. In bacon fat, sauté garlic and shrimp until shrimp turn pink. Stir in lemon juice and green onions.
5. Serve shrimp over cheesy grits, topped with bacon.

**Fried Calamari**

**Ingredients:**

- 1 lb calamari rings
- 1 cup all-purpose flour
- 1 tsp paprika
- Salt and pepper, to taste
- Vegetable oil for frying
- Lemon wedges and marinara sauce, for serving

**Instructions:**

1. Heat oil in a deep fryer or heavy pot to 350°F (175°C).
2. In a bowl, mix flour, paprika, salt, and pepper.
3. Dredge calamari rings in the flour mixture, shaking off excess.
4. Fry in batches for 2-3 minutes until golden and crispy. Drain on paper towels.
5. Serve hot with lemon wedges and marinara sauce.

**Salmon Tartare**

**Ingredients:**

- 8 oz fresh salmon fillet, finely diced
- 1 tbsp capers, chopped
- 1 tbsp red onion, finely diced
- 1 tbsp fresh dill, chopped
- 1 tbsp lemon juice
- 1 tsp Dijon mustard
- 2 tbsp olive oil
- Salt and pepper, to taste
- Toasted baguette slices or crackers, for serving

**Instructions:**

1. In a bowl, combine salmon, capers, red onion, and dill.
2. In a small bowl, whisk lemon juice, mustard, olive oil, salt, and pepper.
3. Pour dressing over salmon mixture and toss gently.
4. Chill for 15 minutes before serving.
5. Serve with toasted baguette slices or crackers.

**Blackened Catfish**

**Ingredients:**

- 4 catfish fillets
- 2 tbsp paprika
- 1 tbsp cayenne pepper
- 1 tbsp garlic powder
- 1 tbsp onion powder
- 1 tsp dried thyme
- 1 tsp dried oregano
- 1 tsp salt
- 1/2 tsp black pepper
- 2 tbsp olive oil
- Lemon wedges, for serving

**Instructions:**

1. In a small bowl, combine paprika, cayenne, garlic powder, onion powder, thyme, oregano, salt, and pepper.
2. Pat catfish fillets dry and rub the spice mix evenly on both sides.
3. Heat olive oil in a heavy skillet over medium-high heat.
4. Cook fillets 3-4 minutes per side until blackened and cooked through.
5. Serve immediately with lemon wedges.

# Seafood Gumbo

## Ingredients:

- 1/2 cup vegetable oil
- 1/2 cup flour
- 1 onion, diced
- 1 bell pepper, diced
- 2 celery stalks, diced
- 4 cloves garlic, minced
- 1 tsp thyme
- 2 bay leaves
- 4 cups seafood stock
- 1 lb shrimp, peeled and deveined
- 1 lb crab meat
- 1/2 lb andouille sausage, sliced
- 1 cup okra, sliced
- Salt and pepper, to taste
- Cooked white rice, for serving
- Chopped green onions and parsley, for garnish

## Instructions:

1. Make a dark roux by whisking flour into hot oil in a large pot, stirring constantly until deep brown (about 15 minutes).

2. Add onion, bell pepper, celery, and garlic; cook until soft.

3. Stir in thyme, bay leaves, and stock. Bring to a simmer.

4. Add sausage and okra; cook 10 minutes.

5. Add shrimp and crab; cook until shrimp are pink, about 5 minutes.

6. Season with salt and pepper. Remove bay leaves.

7. Serve over rice and garnish with green onions and parsley.

## Lobster Salad with Citrus Vinaigrette

### Ingredients:

- 1 lb cooked lobster meat, chopped
- 4 cups mixed salad greens
- 1 avocado, sliced
- 1 orange, peeled and segmented
- 1/4 cup red onion, thinly sliced
- 1/4 cup toasted almonds
- 1/4 cup olive oil
- Juice of 1 lemon
- Juice of 1 orange
- 1 tsp honey
- Salt and pepper, to taste

### Instructions:

1. In a small bowl, whisk olive oil, lemon juice, orange juice, honey, salt, and pepper.
2. In a large bowl, combine greens, avocado, orange segments, red onion, and almonds.
3. Toss with vinaigrette.
4. Top with lobster meat and serve immediately.

**Crab Pasta with Garlic and Herbs**

**Ingredients:**

- 12 oz spaghetti or linguine
- 3 tbsp olive oil
- 4 cloves garlic, minced
- 1/2 tsp red pepper flakes
- 1 cup crab meat
- 1/4 cup fresh parsley, chopped
- Zest and juice of 1 lemon
- Salt and pepper, to taste
- Grated Parmesan, for serving

**Instructions:**

1. Cook pasta according to package instructions. Drain, reserving 1/2 cup pasta water.
2. Heat olive oil in a skillet over medium heat. Add garlic and red pepper flakes; sauté 1-2 minutes.
3. Add crab meat, lemon zest, and juice; cook for 2 minutes.
4. Toss pasta into skillet, adding reserved pasta water as needed to loosen sauce.
5. Stir in parsley, season with salt and pepper.
6. Serve with grated Parmesan.

**Baked Oysters with Parmesan**

**Ingredients:**

- 12 fresh oysters on the half shell
- 1/2 cup grated Parmesan cheese
- 2 cloves garlic, minced
- 1/4 cup breadcrumbs
- 3 tbsp butter, melted
- 2 tbsp fresh parsley, chopped
- Lemon wedges, for serving

**Instructions:**

1. Preheat broiler.
2. In a bowl, mix Parmesan, garlic, breadcrumbs, parsley, and melted butter.
3. Place oysters on a baking sheet. Spoon mixture evenly over each oyster.
4. Broil 3-5 minutes until golden and bubbly.
5. Serve hot with lemon wedges.

## Grilled Shrimp Skewers

### Ingredients:

- 1 lb large shrimp, peeled and deveined
- 3 tbsp olive oil
- 3 cloves garlic, minced
- Juice of 1 lemon
- 1 tsp smoked paprika
- 1/2 tsp chili flakes (optional)
- Salt and pepper, to taste
- Fresh parsley, chopped (for garnish)
- Wooden or metal skewers

### Instructions:

1. In a bowl, combine olive oil, garlic, lemon juice, smoked paprika, chili flakes, salt, and pepper.
2. Add shrimp and toss to coat. Marinate for 15-30 minutes in the fridge.
3. Preheat grill or grill pan over medium-high heat.
4. Thread shrimp onto skewers.
5. Grill for 2-3 minutes per side until shrimp are pink and opaque.
6. Garnish with parsley and serve with lemon wedges.

## Lobster Ravioli

### Ingredients:

- 1 package fresh or frozen lobster ravioli (about 12-16 pieces)
- 3 tbsp butter
- 2 cloves garlic, minced
- 1/2 cup heavy cream
- 1/4 cup grated Parmesan cheese
- 1 tbsp fresh chives, chopped
- Salt and pepper, to taste

### Instructions:

1. Cook ravioli according to package instructions. Drain and set aside.
2. In a skillet, melt butter over medium heat. Add garlic and sauté 1 minute.
3. Stir in heavy cream and bring to a gentle simmer.
4. Add Parmesan, stirring until melted and sauce thickens slightly.
5. Toss ravioli gently in the sauce.
6. Season with salt and pepper. Garnish with chives and serve.

**Pan-Seared Trout**

**Ingredients:**

- 4 trout fillets, skin on
- Salt and pepper, to taste
- 2 tbsp olive oil
- 2 tbsp butter
- 2 cloves garlic, smashed
- 1 lemon, sliced
- Fresh thyme or dill sprigs

**Instructions:**

1. Pat trout dry and season with salt and pepper.
2. Heat olive oil in a large skillet over medium-high heat.
3. Place trout fillets skin-side down, pressing gently to prevent curling. Cook 4-5 minutes until skin is crispy.
4. Flip fillets, add butter, garlic, lemon slices, and herbs to the pan.
5. Spoon melted butter over fish and cook another 2-3 minutes until cooked through.
6. Serve with pan juices spooned on top.

## Seafood Casserole

### Ingredients:

- 1/2 lb shrimp, peeled and deveined
- 1/2 lb scallops
- 1/2 lb white fish (like cod), cut into chunks
- 1 cup cooked pasta (penne or shells)
- 1 cup heavy cream
- 1 cup shredded mozzarella or Gruyère cheese
- 1/2 cup grated Parmesan
- 1/2 cup chopped onions
- 2 cloves garlic, minced
- 1/2 cup white wine
- 2 tbsp butter
- 1 tbsp olive oil
- Salt and pepper, to taste
- Fresh parsley, chopped for garnish

### Instructions:

1. Preheat oven to 375°F (190°C).
2. Heat olive oil and butter in a skillet over medium heat. Sauté onions and garlic until translucent.

3. Add white wine and cook until reduced by half.

4. Stir in heavy cream and bring to simmer. Season with salt and pepper.

5. Add seafood and cook gently for 2 minutes (they will finish cooking in the oven).

6. In a baking dish, combine cooked pasta and seafood mixture. Top with mozzarella and Parmesan.

7. Bake uncovered for 15-20 minutes until bubbly and golden.

8. Garnish with parsley and serve hot.

## Smoked Trout Dip

### Ingredients:

- 8 oz smoked trout, skin removed and flaked
- 4 oz cream cheese, softened
- 1/4 cup sour cream or Greek yogurt
- 1 tbsp lemon juice
- 1 tbsp fresh dill, chopped
- 1 tbsp capers, drained and chopped
- 1 small shallot, minced
- Salt and pepper, to taste
- Crackers or sliced baguette, for serving

### Instructions:

1. In a medium bowl, mix cream cheese and sour cream until smooth.
2. Fold in smoked trout, lemon juice, dill, capers, and shallot.
3. Season with salt and pepper.
4. Chill for at least 30 minutes to blend flavors.
5. Serve with crackers or bread slices.